23rd Edition

FRANCIS POULENC

SONATA

for

Piano, Four Hands

or

Two Pianos

1. Prelude
2. Rustique
3. Final

CHESTER MUSIC

(A division of Music Sales Limited)
14/15 Berners Street, London, W1T 3LJ

à Mademoiselle Simone Tilliard.

SONATE.

Piano Four Hands.

I. PRELUDE.

Revised Edition by the composer 1939.

Francis Poulenc.
(1918)

Chester Music Limited, 14/15 Berners Street, London, W1T 3LJ
Copyright renewd in U.S.A. 1948

CH02907

5 5

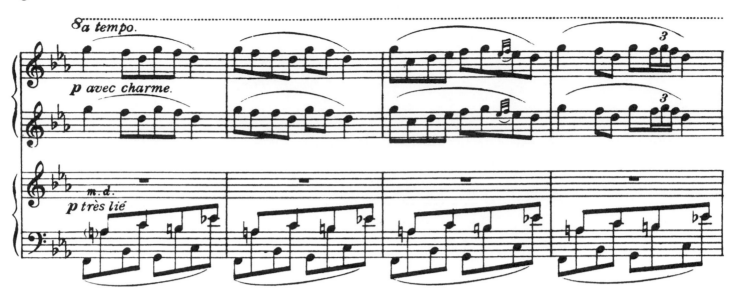

8

très lié (les appoggiatures très sonores.)

— subito *pp quasi trille*

Presto. strident.

ralentir un peu.

(respirer
longuement)

II. RUSTIQUE.

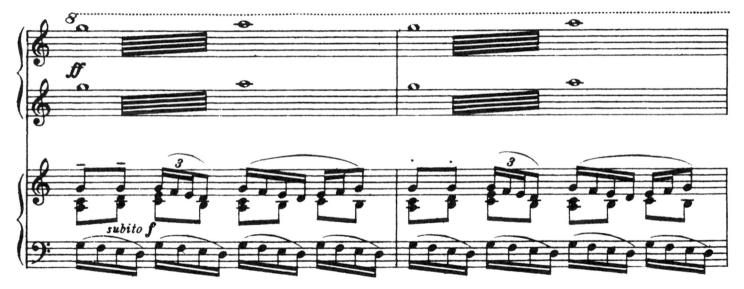

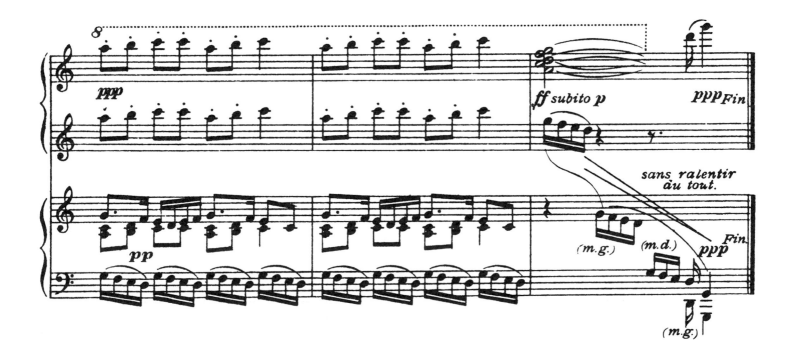

III. FINAL.

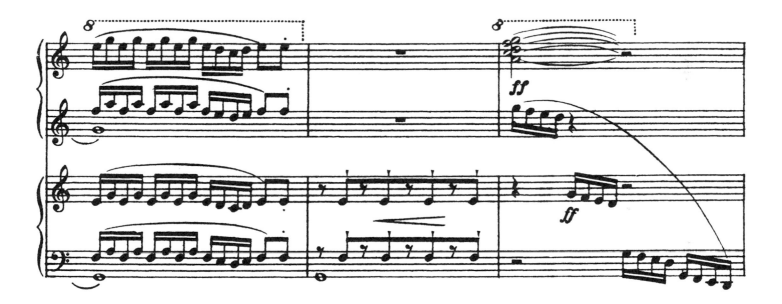

16

8va bassa..

augmenter   peu   à   peu

8va bassa...:loco.

Commencer à s'apaiser et à diminuer.

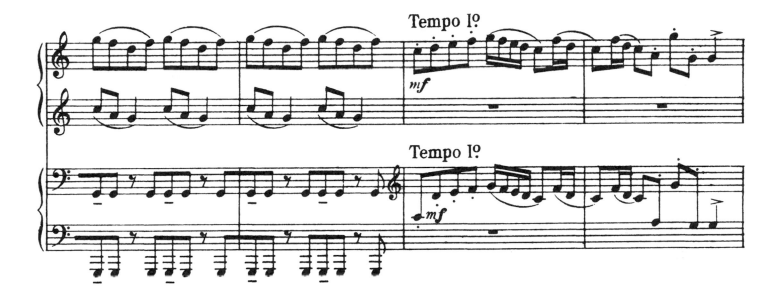

Tempo I?

Tempo I?

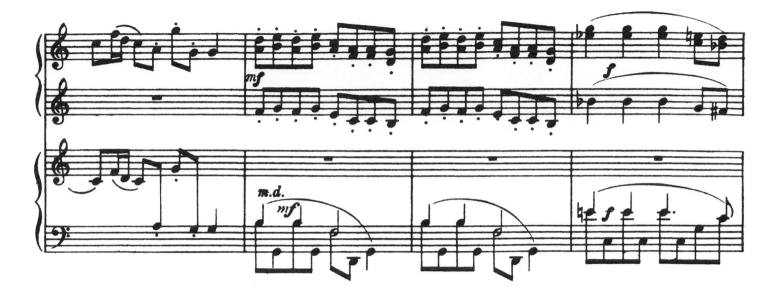

Boulogne sur Seine, Juin 1918.